JEFFREY W. AUBUCHON

Put Your Toe in the Pacific

A Friend's Wisdom

92252 PRESS

First published by 92252 Press 2021

The views expressed herein belong solely to Jeffrey W. Aubuchon, who has no binding relationship—ministerial or otherwise—with Saint Anselm Abbey. The author has neither sought nor secured ecclesiastical endorsement of this book.

Readers' reviews are vital to independent authors. Please consider reviewing this book on Amazon.com to advise readers like you. Other books from Jeffrey W. Aubuchon and 92252 Press include:

Three Desert Stories (2019)

Flight School (2020)

When Coronavirus Unmapped the Peace Corps' Journey (2021)

Learn more at jeffreywaubuchon.com and on Twitter @JeffreyAubuchon

First edition

ISBN: 978-1-73-405926-7

This book was professionally typeset on Reedsy. Find out more at reedsy.com

In Memoriam

Father Michael H. Custer, O.S.B.
1910-2006

Monk—Teacher—Friend

"[T]here is a good zeal which separates from vices and leads to God
and to life everlasting. This zeal, therefore, the monks should
practice with the most fervent love."
Rule for Monks, Chapter 72

Preface

Like many first-semester students, I struggled to find my place in the new college world, even though studying in the woods of New Hampshire differed little from growing up in the woods of Massachusetts. I busied myself during the day by studying and working, but evenings felt lonely. Early in September, I decided to attend the daily Mass celebrated by the monks at Saint Anselm College followed by dinner in the cafeteria. My strategy worked: I found like-minded students who became lifelong friends, I learned from the monks—many of whom have also remained in my life—and by the time Christmas break arrived, I wanted to stay at school rather than return home. The daily routine comforted me and many of the relationships I formed became part of the life I built at Saint Anselm and after.

Among all the monks I met at Saint Anselm, none became as close a friend as Father Michael Custer. While we shared some things in common, ours was an unlikely friendship: he was 89 and retired while I was just 19 and starting my sophomore year. He had taught chemistry (and never let anyone forget it) while I studied history. As I grew eager to see the wider world, Father Michael often reminded me that he had never traveled "farther than Pinardville," the College's neighborhood in Goffstown, N.H. Yet, from our meeting in the fall of 1999 until his death on May 1, 2006, we shared a friendship that I have kept as a model for others in my adult life. I've noticed three peculiarities about our time together.

First, and perhaps most obviously, the seventy-year gap in our ages set our friendship apart. Yet, aside from his dated cultural references to Elvis Presley, Lawrence Welk, and Katharine Hepburn, the seventy years never got in the way of our friendship but enriched it.

Second, many loved Father Michael for the stories he told in conversation, in his homilies, and in his correspondence. He kept his stories in a loose-leaf binder that I helped him digitize and bind into a more permanent product, now housed in the College's Geisel Library (BX1756.C8 S8 2000). I include a handful of these stories in the current short project—the rest stand for themselves on the library's shelves and need no embellishment from me. At the heart of this book are some of the forty letters I saved from our exchange. In rereading the letters to prepare for this project during the pandemic year of 2020-2021, I could hear his soft and reassuring voice with its perfectly timed inflection points. Indeed, Father Michael told a story as well as Scheherazade; in my writing, I hope to match his dexterity in delivering a punchline (or a parenthetical tickle).

Last, ours became friendship for friendship's sake. Father Michael never acted as a spiritual director to me, nor did he ever hear my confession. We did, however, listen to the other's stories—often ending in laughter. How blessed are the thousands, like me, who called Father Michael a friend.

This book is not a biography, although I included his own "autobiography" in Part II. I have digitized Father Michael's touching obituary written by Abbot Matthew Leavy, O.S.B. and posted it to my website at jeffreywaubuchon.com along with another story I found among his letters. Many people—especially his brother monks and his chemistry disciples—surely remember more about Father Michael's life and habits than I do. Just a sample of his letters and my recollections follow in these pages, memories that speak to the atypical nature of our friendship. While you read, and after you've chuckled at his clever phrases, I urge you to think about both the conventional and unconventional friendships in your life and the ways to nurture those relationships.

I have tried to use as many of Father Michael's own words in the book as mine, and I have differentiated his expressions with italics as well as given him the final words of the book. I do not claim to work as a stenographer and, while I have recounted the conversations as I remember, I acknowledge having a quite imperfect memory.

I am grateful to the friends who helped create this book: Benjamin Tautges who snapped the cover photo in Santa Barbara and Anna Burrous who expertly turned the photo into a cover. John Flanagan and my 2002 classmate, Julia Parodi Mitchell, critiqued early drafts.

Two decades have passed since I graduated from Saint Anselm College. Since then, I've remained thankful both for the College and the monastic community for the unshakable foundation they gave me as I set out into the world as a young adult. I have, in turn, shared this knowledge with my students, including some who have attended Saint Anselm themselves. In gratitude for the many gifts I received between 1998 and 2002, I am donating all of the after-tax profit from this book to the Father Michael Custer Scholarship Fund at the College so that not only will Father Michael's love of chemistry live on in future generations of students, but so will his friendly wisdom.

June 5, 2021
Sausalito, California

Prologue

"There you are, Father Daniel. That book is yours for the semester."

"Thank you, Jeff. Look at this script," the bearded monk said, cracking open the book of illuminated manuscripts. "Notice the detail and colors; they are beauty from a brush."

"Truly," I said.

"They don't even teach cursive in school anymore. Alack and alas," Father Daniel retorted, feigning a sigh and snapping the book shut. "See you soon."

He took the book under his hand and turned away from the library circulation desk, walking toward the doors. Father Daniel always reminded me of jolly Friar Tuck, but in a Benedictine habit. When he stepped outside, the tower bells intoned five, marking my shift's end.

"You know all the monks, Jeff," said the library supervisor, Diana, as I packed my things.

"Most of them, I guess. I don't know them all. I only know Father Daniel from campus ministry."

"He's a clever one, that Father Daniel," Diana said in her English accent.

"I don't know that old monk, the one who walks around Alumni Hall, always bundled up."

"Which? And be careful when you specify old."

"I think his name is Father Michael. He wears a knit cap."

"He's a sweet man. I believe he taught chemistry, although I don't know him well. He doesn't come in here often. You should send him an email. Introduce yourself. You're bold enough."

"You think so?" I asked. "I mean, he's good with email?"

"I remember a story in the *Crier* about his use of email. He jokes about knowing computers so well. It won't hurt you to try."

"I'll think about it," I said when the bells began to peel from the tower of Alumni Hall, the ivy-clad edifice that had served as the first college. The 5:05 bells reminded the campus community every evening that Mass would begin in ten minutes. "See you Thursday, Diana."

From the stout brick library, I walked under the leafy trees and across the campus driveway to climb the granite steps and open the colossal wooden doors of the Abbey Church. As my eyes adjusted to the dim light, I smelled the faint, lingering smell of incense. No matter how many chapels or cathedrals I visit around the world, none suggest both beauty and belonging as the cylindrical all-brick Abbey Church with its three colossal stained glass windows depicting the persons of Trinity. I walked through the nave and climbed the sanctuary stairs into the choir where the monks celebrate daily Mass. The multicolored clerestory windows of the choir reflect the many emotions of the Psalms, sung by the monks four times each day from their stalls.

A handful of students, faculty, and community members join the monks each evening for Mass. Some of the simple hymns still ring in my head as I think of the solemn fathers filing in with the young ones in the front and senior priests at the rear. I knew some of the young monks well and considered them friends while most of the older monks—like Father Daniel—were professors and a bit more intimidating, at least to a young student. Towards the very end of the procession walk the oldest, and almost ancient, monks with the abbot; their faces careworn from many years of service to the Abbey and College.

Father Michael stood shorter than most, with a bald head and fringe of white hair around his ears. He moved slowly but determinedly with a bit of a slouch and, despite his almost elvish appearance, he expressed holiness in his gentle way. That's all I knew of him in the fall of my second year.

Saint Anselm Abbey Church with bell tower behind.

I

Beginnings

*"Listen carefully, my child, to your master's precepts,
and incline the ear of your heart."*

Rule for Monks, Prologue

Meeting

My family only connected to the Internet just before the turn of this Millennium. I never used email before college and, in those days, the college used a network-based system that required logging on to a campus computer to read my messages. The era surely lacked the convenience of the smart phone. I decided to introduce myself to Father Michael as Diana suggested and figured a short message would be a good salvo:

> Dear Father Michael,
>
> I am a sophomore here at the College and I see you at daily Mass. I hear you are good with computers, so I thought I would try to reach you by email. It would be nice to meet you at your convenience.
>
> Sincerely,
> Jeff Aubuchon

I received an equally-brief reply the next day. I wish I saved a copy, but this is what I recall:

> *Dear Jeff:*
>
> *I am glad to meet you. When I came to St. Anselm*

College we had cows, not computers. Now we do many
things by computers but have no cows. If you would like to
visit sometime, I am in my office almost every afternoon
in the basement of Gadbois Hall, the nurse's building. You
can find me there.
　Father Michael

I had no classes on Friday afternoon and decided to find his office then. I did not, however, respond to the email to avoid committing myself to the visit.

I had taken some history classes on the first and second floors of Gadbois Hall, but I never followed the stairs into the basement. Not surprisingly, it looked much like the upstairs corridors except slightly darker and, if I remember correctly, offices and lab spaces replaced classrooms on the bottom floor. The office doors with their engraved nameplates all stood closed on that Friday afternoon, except for one that I found cracked ajar with a faded, paper sign from a dot matrix printer that read "Father Michael, OSB." I looked through the open crack before knocking.

An old television—the kind I had as a kid in the 1980s—played a muted football game. The TV sat on a cart with an enormous VCR player and old video cassettes with faded labels littered the whole thing. I heard a deep cough that moved phlegm. Light came in through the small windows at the front wall, the kind of arrangement where you could see ankles pass by on the sidewalk above. I knocked and heard another cough.

Come in.

"Father Michael?" I asked timidly as I opened the door and saw him sitting in an armchair.

You must be Jeff. Email Jeff. Here, sit down, he said as he sat up and motioned for me to sit in a smaller chair beside his desk. He wore his black habit and collar with an old, navy blue cardigan. As I returned the door to its cracked position, I noticed his heavy coat—the same he wore around campus—on the door's hook.

The cluttered office perfectly fit an emeritus professor with its mess of yellowed papers, articles, and books, never sorted in his retirement. A Bunsen burner, or perhaps a hot plate, with a beaker of water boiled on his desk. The beaker logically belonged to a chemistry professor, but I could not understand its purpose as it boiled away without his attention. His cough suggested some congestion—perhaps the water added some moisture to his office.

Now Email Jeff, where are you from?

"Ashburnham. In Massachusetts. It's a small town."

What's it near? I know Massachusetts.

"Fitchburg,"

I know Fitchburg. I'm from Lowell, what they call the Venice of America.

In my mind, I tried to unravel his claim. I didn't know Lowell well, but I remembered the canals.

What do you study?

"History."

You can't do much with history except teach. Chemistry is a very good major. Some will teach and others will develop new chemicals, but you can always find a job with chemistry.

"I'm not very good with numbers or formulas," I said. "But I like reading and writing about history. I think I might like to teach history."

That's good, then. A good history teacher will give his students good stories. I always preached with stories. It's good to know some stories, they make the class interesting for the students. Look here, he said, pulling a dusty picture in a thin eight-by-ten-inch frame from his desk.

Someone snapped the black and white photo from the sanctuary of the Abbey Church. The preacher—the bald head surely belonged to him—kept his back to the camera while nurses wearing white uniforms filled the front rows of the church. He pointed to the photo. *I always taught the nurses, and I always preached at their Pinning Mass.* I held the photo for a moment before returning it to the pile of papers on his desk. My thumbprint remained on the dusty glass.

Father Michael asked about my parents and my siblings and, in turn, told me about his family of musicians and their summers on Cape Cod. The conversation flowed effortlessly as he surely had shared hundreds of such conversations before.

Now, I'll tell you the same story I told to the students at the last student Mass I said. You have to be clever to hold their attention, and quick or else you'll lose them, he explained, before continuing:

> *A king went hunting in India and found a baby tiger abandoned by its mother. The king took the tiger up in his arms, brought it home, and gave it to his son as a gift. The prince and the tiger grew up together and they loved each other. Even when the tiger was fully grown, the prince could wrestle with him. One day, while they were wrestling, the prince cut his finger; when the tiger tasted blood, he tore the young man apart.*

He paused, savoring the cliffhanger he had made.

Students all have that tiger inside them. Don't ever let him taste blood or he will tear you apart. Drugs, sex, alcohol may be in a young person's blood. Don't let that tiger taste it.

He smiled and coughed again as he sat back in his chair.

Stories. Teach them using stories, Jeff. Now come back and see us again some afternoon. I will be here.

He extended his hand, which I shook as I stood up.

"Thank you, Father Michael," I said as I slipped out of the office into the darkened hallway.

I did return, and I spent many Friday afternoons with Father Michael.

"Now remember gentlemen, be very careful in this experiment. We can always replace the students! It's the equipment that's hard to get." The Tower (St. Anselm Coll.), vol. XV, no. 3, 22 Nov. 1946.

Gaudium

I didn't think to share any news with Father Michael during my summer vacation, but I enjoyed my newfound confidence: college suited me. I enjoyed my studies, and while I found my summer work and travels pleasing, I eagerly anticipated returning to campus in late August. My enthusiasm for school grew when I received an unexpected letter from Father Michael by mail.

July 19, 2000

Dear Jeff:

As you perhaps know, on Sunday, July 9th I passed out at morning prayers and was taken to the hospital in an ambulance. Three or four heart doctors were working on me (I hope my insurance is paid up) and at first they thought I needed a heart pacer. After final consultation, they all agreed that I did not need the heart pacer, that I should wear support hose and use lots of salt.

On Monday, July 24th, I will be leaving for Plymouth to spend a week down at the waterfront. The pastor sent word today that I should come, and that he has notified the parishioners that I am coming. He has me preach to them my last day in Plymouth.

I also hope to visit with Doctor Currie that week. He has a house beside the Kennedy Compound at Hyannis Port. He has been after me to visit with him for some time. This summer I hope to visit with him.

Other than that, things are very quiet here on campus.

I just wanted you to know that I will be leaving on Monday, the 24th for the week. You will excuse me now as I have to pack.

Father Michael

I did not know about his episode at morning prayers, nor did I know he planned to travel to Plymouth. I felt special that he made the effort to tell me. Reading his letter, I understood that I was more than a student with an ID number; indeed, he remembered me even during vacations.

When I returned to campus, I emailed Father Michael to see if it would be convenient to visit him on that first Friday. He said yes, but also asked to meet in the front sitting room of the monastery rather than at his office in Gadbois Hall. I don' think I returned to his office again; instead, we sat in the front parlor for our Friday afternoon chats. When I arrived, I saw he had a new walker by his side, which explained the change in location.

"That's quite the cart they've given you," I said referring to his walker, trying to make light of it. The sturdy walker had wheels and handbrakes, and doubled as a seat if needed. Someone had added a basket that he filled with an assortment of papers—much like his office—as well as mounted a bicycle horn and a small U.S. flag to the handle bar. The aesthetic could not have looked any more his own.

It takes me where I need to go. Very convenient for carrying things.

After sharing stories from our respective summer travels, him to Plymouth and me to Dallas, he asked about the new semester.

Are any subjects giving you trouble this year?

"Medieval Latin," I blurted without hesitation. "I did ok in the first two years, but these translations are harder to understand."

With Latin, if you look at it you can usually get the idea. Greek, on the other hand—he trailed off for a bit, shaking his head—*I could never make heads or tails of it.* We both started to chuckle.

"How much Greek did you have to study?" I asked.

Enough to finish seminary. I knew my vocation was God's will when I passed that last semester of Greek. Kyrie *this and* Christe *that,* he said as we started to chuckle. *You'll do ok in Latin, like I did in Greek. But it's almost time for Mass now, please excuse me.*

I stood with him and helped him with his walker.

"I'll walk with you to church if that's ok."

Quite fine.

We walked through the monastery corridor to the Church and parted at the sacristy.

"See you soon," I whispered.

I hope. And you know, you wouldn't need much Latin if you studied chemistry.

He walked on into the sacristy before I could reply.

* * *

A card from Father Michael awaited me at home when I returned for Christmas. The watercolor religious image on the front, painted by Father Iain, again reminded me that Father Michael and the other monks prayed daily for their students and alumni. In return, I tried to find Father Michael a silly card about Santa rather than a religious motif, a practice I continued each Christmas. While he never commented on them, I suspect he appreciated the humor of reindeer droppings or workshop elves demanding union protections amid the many images of holy families and heralding angels he received. Of all the Christmas cards I saved from Father Michael, I think this one from 2005 is my favorite for its simplicity:

May the Infant Savior, born of the Virgin Mary,

comfort us all in the light of His coming,

this holy season of Christmas

and throughout the New Year.

With sincere appreciation for Many Past Kindnesses

Father Michael

'05

Gifts

A
t the beginning of the new semester, I received a letter explaining my election to Delta Epsilon Sigma, the national honor society of Catholic college students. The letter indicated I could bring a guest to the induction ceremony scheduled for a Sunday afternoon in the Cardinal Cushing Student Center. The long drive would inconvenience my parents for an hour-long ceremony, so I invited Father Michael instead.

I've never been invited to an honor society ceremony, I better accept, he told me with a bit of a laugh.

"Thank you. I will pick you up in my red car outside the church," I told him. He agreed.

Although the Cushing Center is not much farther from the Abbey than his basement office, Father Michael had started to slow down with his walker, so I thought driving would be prudent, especially in the cold.

A snowstorm blustered through New Hampshire on the day of the ceremony and arranging the short ride around the campus quad proved wise. I did not confirm the details of the day with Father Michael because I knew he would not miss it. My red car crawled up the snowy campus driveway behind a blue Chevy Malibu. As I approached the the Abbey Church, I saw him bundled in his parka and knit hat, making his way down the stairs, which still needed shoveling. His left hand grasped his walking stick and his right hand held his scarf over his mouth. To my surprise, I watched him open the door to the blue Malibu—rather than my red Ford—even though I arrived minutes earlier than I arranged. I jumped out.

"Father Michael!" I shouted and waved. The falling snow muffled my shout.

Oh Jeff, he said, and shut the door to the Malibu before walking towards my car. I opened the passenger door and helped to get him and his walking stick in the warm car.

They are going to the same event and offered me a lift. I didn't want to disappoint them, he told me.

With Father Michael secured, I turned left towards the brick three-story Hilary Hall at the foot of the quad, and then right towards the brick Cushing Center.

I remember when Hilary Hall was the only dormitory on campus. We built it well because it's still in use and very popular. Now, leave me here and park the car. I will meet you inside, he instructed as he let himself out. Like a good student, I followed his directions.

I recall little of that ceremony, only sitting next to Father Michael and watching the snowfall outside of the lounge windows. At the end, he handed me a small white box pulled from his coat pocket. *I've never been to one of these,* he reminded me, *but I believe a small gift is customary.*

He gave me a rosary, the same rosary photographed on the front cover of this book. The beads included a curious crucifix designed for the Millennium celebrations, which helps remind me of the date all these years later.

To say your prayers with. Now, I think I'll go back up to the monastery if you wouldn't mind driving.

"Thank you, Father Michael. I'll go get the car. The red car. Wait for me," I reminded him as he bundled himself.

* * *

By the time of the winter ceremony, I had found confidence in my chosen career as a history teacher, which I must have mentioned in my thank you note following the event given Father Michael's response:

April 27, 2001

Dear Jeff:

My sincere appreciation for your nice long letter, and nice to know that you will be with us for another year.

You do very well financially in teaching, it is too bad you do not have a teaching job during the summer months. But I do hope you can get something worthwhile during the summer months. How well college students do in the summer depends on the cost of their room and board, which at times is very expensive.

Yes, we enjoyed our work during the summer down on Cape Cod. But we did not do very well financially, it was during the Great Days of the Depression of 1929. After working all summer, I think I came home with three hundred dollars. You could make that by teaching four days. But spending all summer on the Cape with room and board was not too bad.

I hope you can find a summer job that will be near enough to your girlfriend so you can visit quite often. Our family orchestra was offered a job at a hotel in Martha's Vineyard, but my brothers did not want to go there as they

would be too far away from their girlfriends for the whole
summer. I would have loved to spend the summer on that
island off the Cape. And, financially, I would have done
much better than a bellhop, and perhaps as much fun.

Have an enjoyable summer, and come back with lots of
zeal.

Father Michael

Come back with lots of zeal. Zeal is not a word often used in
contemporary conversation, but Father Michael knew it well
from Chapter 72 of St. Benedict's *Rule*. St. Benedict understood
zeal not only as enthusiasm or energy; rather, he described zeal
as the loving disposition towards which all people of faith should
aim.

St. Benedict's—and maybe Father Michael's—understanding
of zeal probably does not resonate with most American college
students today. In rereading his letter, and rereading St. Benedict's own words, I wonder if Father Michael hoped to cultivate
this maturity in me. We never discussed a monastic vocation,
nor did he offer anything but praise towards my girlfriend, but
through his use of simple stories, well-chosen words, and by
leading an exemplary life, Father Michael certainly put me on a
path oriented towards a zealous life in a secular world, and I am
grateful.

* * *

"My grandmother has declined in health," I told him one rainy
afternoon in the monastery parlor. "I don't know if the doctors
will offer her more treatment."

Is that so? I could give her St. Maurus' Blessing. If you can give me a lift in your red car.

Father Michael had mentioned the blessing a few times in passing but, given my good health and youthfulness, I suppose I hadn't paid it much attention.

"How does it work?"

Saint Maurus was a monk and disciple of Saint Benedict who possessed the gift of miracles. Maurus used a piece of the True Cross to bless and cure many and started our tradition of blessing the sick with the Cross.

"Do you have a piece of the True Cross?" I asked.

Yes, it was a gift at my ordination. Cardinal Cushing ordained two of us that day and he gave me the relic and the other fellow a chalice. I got the better deal because you can only do so much with a chalice. Father Michael let out a chuckle. *But it's not just for me. The others know it is on my desk. They borrow it to give the blessing as needed.*

"What does it do?"

It doesn't always do what we want it to do, but it always does something. It gives comfort and peace, sometimes other things. I would happily bless your grandmother and I will pray for her in the meantime.

"Thank you," I said. "I am glad for that."

We spoke on several occasions about traveling to Massachusetts to visit my grandparents, but the opportunity never came. Still, I found comfort in knowing he held her in the light during her final months.

That summer, Father Michael permanently moved to the Bishop Peterson Residence, a nursing home for elderly priests in New Hampshire, just a ten-minute ride from campus. There, in his cozy nursing home room, the next phase of our friendship unfolded during my senior year of college and afterward.

A Year of Change

September 10, 2001

Dear Jeff:

It was nice having you here for a visit this afternoon. It gave me an opportunity for thanking you for the lovely postcards that you sent from Texas. I do hope that I will be present at your wedding, I hope you have a friend with a car who could pick me up.

You had an opportunity to see my lovely room here at the nursing home, and to meet some of the staff. It is a long day here at the residence and anything out of the ordinary is exciting, like lightning striking the building twice during the same storm. When lightning strikes, the fire alarm rings, lights are flashing, and the fire doors close automatically. No one can turn the alarm off, only the firemen when they come. And they send extra apparatus when the alarm is for a nursing home or hospital. The firemen left and were back again in ten minutes when lightning struck a second time, and everything was repeated again. There may be a piece of metal on the roof that acts as a lightning rod and attracts the lightning. When lightning strikes here, you know it because the whole building seems to shake. No one was hurt and there was no damage to the building, so I think all the patients enjoyed the excitement.

Last week, Father Aquinas came and said, 'get your things on, we are going up to the camp.' Our camp is on Squam Lake (the Golden Pond) and after being confined to the nursing home, any ride is exciting. We went out in the boat and a bald eagle flew over our heads. The abbot and some of the novices were there for the week. We had lunch on a large table, on the porch overlooking the lake. It was a lovely outing for Brother Thomas and myself.

And you will not have to go around looking for someone for the Junior Prom.

Father Michael

The date of this letter arrests me. I don't remember visiting Father Michael on Monday, September 10 but the events of the next morning—Tuesday, September 11, 2001—remain in my mind. I watched both towers collapse while I worked at the library circulation desk. Classes were canceled and much of our community filed into the Abbey Church for a special noontime Mass. We found comfort in each other and hoped for peace.

I suspect that was the only week in which I visited Father Michael twice. His letter indicates a visit on Monday and I know I returned to the nursing home on Friday, September 14. A professor invited me to worship that evening at nearby Temple Israel and I decided to visit Father Michael in the late afternoon. I suppose I sought peace and understanding that week like many in our strange new world.

I only ever saw Father Michael angry that one afternoon.

Perhaps I visited him looking for answers from a wise, old master. Yet, I found him just as human and confused as any of us. One line from our conversation remains with me all these years later. Of the jihadists, he said: *they think they will see Allah, but I think their god will be red with horns.*

I'm saddened when I think back to his anger. In the years since, I lived in a Muslim country and, as I have matured, I've learned we cannot always understand or explain the world around us in simple terms. Of course, I don't think the jihadists were destined for Paradise, but I also don't equate the Islamic understanding of God with the devil. I don't fault Father Michael for his frank and casual comments even though I disagree with them, but I recall them as surprisingly uncharacteristic.

* * *

Father Michael held Michaelmas—the feast of St. Michael and the Archangels on September 29—as an important day; I now mark it myself since I returned from studying in Wales. The British and Irish traditionally start their fall academic term on that day. In folklore, clear weather on Michaelmas foreshadows a long winter, as the rhyme notes: "Michaelmas Day be bright and clear, there will be two winters in the year." Michaelmas 2001 was bright with blue skies and a perfectly autumnal temperature of sixty degrees, proverbially suggesting a prolonged, double winter.

The Archangel Michael is one of the rare Biblical figures that exist in the Jewish Old Testament, Christian New Testament, and Muslim Qur'an. Michael acted as the great protector of the Jewish people while the Christian tradition holds he will lead God's armies against those of Satan in the end times. Muslims consider Mika'il as a close friend and messenger of Allah.

I don't know how Father Michael came by the name when he entered the monastery to replace his baptismal name of Herbert. Father Michael certainly didn't look like the chiseled, sword-wielding Archangel of icons, and I think his gentleness would have been better captured as a cherubic guardian angel. In either case, Father Michael acted as a caring soul who looked after others. The old prayer popularized by Pope Leo XIII, which Father Michael knew well, invokes his namesake St. Michael as a protector from the start: *Saint Michael the Archangel, Defend us in battle....*

While calling on Father Michael for help expressed less drama than the prayer suggests, he always offered wise counsel, fervent prayers, and good humor to anyone in need, not only in September but year-round.

* * *

Completing my graduation requirements and student teaching challenged me enough in the 2001-2002 school year, but I also added a wedding and finding a job to my list of tasks.

The wedding preparations hold little space in my memory. I bought the rings, arranged the cars, and taste-tested the food. We shared a desire for a smaller wedding, with Mass in the Abbey Church and the reception at a nearby inn. As family members were traveling from Texas for both graduation and a wedding, we decided to celebrate both events during the same week: we would graduate on May 18 and marry on May 25.

I remember a bit more about my job search. I luckily fell into a teaching position at the school where I completed my student teaching but I questioned if I truly wanted to stay. My friend and history professor, Father William, had served as headmaster of the Woodside Priory School near San Francisco for many years. He encouraged me to visit the Bay Area during spring break and arranged meetings and interviews for me at the school. At twenty-one years old, I was headed to California for the first time, and I eagerly wanted to tell Father Michael about it.

They say Woodside is a nice place, but I've never been.

"I'm looking forward to seeing the school."

I worried we were reaching too far when the monks started talking about taking on the responsibility of that priory in California, but the school does well on its own out there. And we had some experience with our prep school here on campus years ago. They say it costs more to go to that prep school than the College. Can you imagine?

"I hear everything is more expensive in California."

They do say that. I hope you will see some sights while you're there, like the trolley cars or the Golden Bridge. Be sure to put your toe in the Pacific for me as I'll never have the chance now.

"I will, and I'll try to send a postcard with a nice picture of the ocean."

Yes, please do. You know how I love the shore. Something different to look at is always much appreciated. When you return, I will tell you the story of Father Damien of Molokai, the Pacific priest.

* * *

I'm uncertain if I sent a postcard, but I did save an email Father Michael sent not too long after my return. I reminded him of the wedding and he responded:

May 17, 2002
Dear Jeff:

Yes. I look forward to attending this wedding. And I will be here whenever they come to pick me up.

And would also enjoy a visit, so we can talk about the trip to California.

Your graduation is tomorrow. I do hope the weather holds up so you can have the ceremony outside.

Father Michael

The Michaelmas forecast of a double winter proved true when snow fell again on Saturday, May 18, 2002, moving graduation indoors from the snow-dusted campus quad. Nonetheless, I delighted in knowing Father Michael thought of me downtown at the Peterson as I closed that beautiful chapter of my education in the campus gym.

As early as his September 10 letter, Father Michael asked for a friend to pick him up at the Peterson Residence in time for the wedding. Every time he mentioned it I said my groomsman, Corey, would collect him.

Is he a classmate? Where's he from?

"He is," I said, "from Nashua."

Good people in Nashua, close to Lowell, he said before adding: *I suppose he studies history, too?*

Corey had studied history, and could certainly transport Father Michael himself. I decided, however, to give Father Michael a little surprise by accompanying them from the Residence to the Abbey. I asked Corey to drive, and we dressed in our tuxedos for the trip across town in my red car.

We found Father Michael waiting on a bench in the reception area, dressed and pressed for the wedding. He laughed and shook his head when we entered in our long coats.

I said just to send a car, he shook his head and chuckled. *The groom is too busy to come himself. This must be Corey from Nashua.* As always, Father Michael extended his hand to shake Corey's.

I introduced them while Father Michael scanned the corridor.

I will introduce you to some of the other residents now, Father Michael said as we began to slowly walk down the hall and away from the front door. I think he felt a bit special that we were all dressed to collect him, and we were happy to meet some of the other residents, many of whom I met before. He walked as tall and straight as he could, pushing his walker and undoubtedly feeling like the man of the hour. I gladly shared in his happiness.

We do receive visitors here, but not dressed like that, he told us with a laugh.

"We should get going, Father Michael, we don't want the wedding to start without us."

That's true, he said in serious agreement, as he put on his Roy Orbison sunglasses.

Corey pulled the little red car to the curb and opened the passenger door. He took the walker from Father Michael so that I could help him sit. I felt relieved he wore pants instead of a habit as it made the movement a bit easier for us all. I got him settled as Corey shut the trunk with the folded walker inside.

"Ready?" Corey asked before we got in the car.

"More like exhausted. I think this was the biggest challenge of the day, Corey." We both laughed before we hopped inside, with Corey at the wheel and me in the back, and set off for the College from which we had both just graduated.

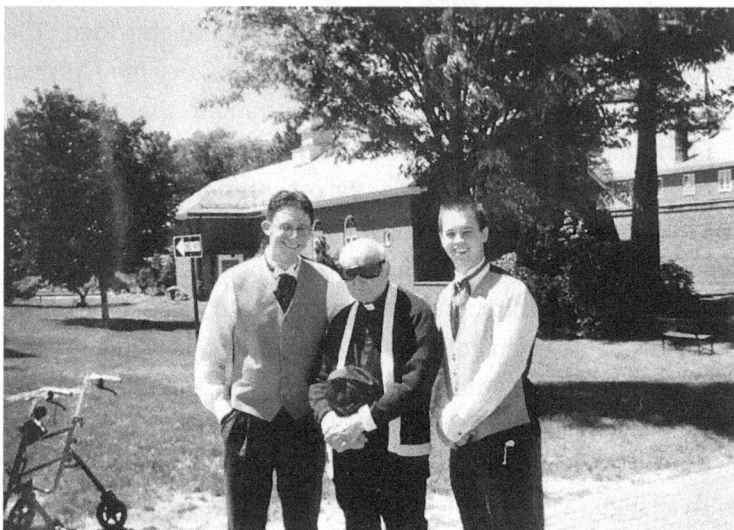

Father Michael wore his white alb and stole to concelebrate the Mass, even though he sat in the choir stalls with his aged confrere Father Finbar while the other concelebrants gathered around the altar. I couldn't see him from my seat, but the photographer captured one great image of him during the liturgy, showing him totally engaged in the prayers and blessings despite having a "back row" seat. In all his priestly years, I wonder how many weddings Father Michael celebrated, and yet, mine seemed just as special to him as any other.

After the Mass, we received our guests in the cloister yard and I still remember when the arched church door opened and through it came a beaming Father Michael pushing his walker, perhaps oblivious to the line that formed to greet us. The small crowd did not deter him and made his way straight to my parents with a big grin. None of the well-wishers would dare complain he jumped ahead given how happy he looked. I have no idea what they discussed, but I do recall it as a moment of pure joy that I gratefully shared with my family and my friend. I also remember the old Irish advice he offered me, which I later found among his stories.

* * *

In Ireland, if you ask someone where a certain town is located, a native will tell you it is over the next hill. When you get there you will not find the town, but someone will tell you that it is over the next hill. Again, you will not find the town but someone will tell you it is over yet another hill and so on until you actually do come to the town. Why did the first one not tell you where you would find the town? It is because he was afraid you would become discouraged and he knows that if you go over enough hills, you will eventually get there.

Now that is what we must do in married life, take each day at a time, climb each hill together—as they sing in "The Sound of Music"—and begin each hill with a prayer to God.

* * *

When I visited Father Michael after our honeymoon, I reported that I found California beautiful. I saw both leafy palm trees and the giant redwoods. I drove across the Golden Gate Bridge and watched sea lions swim in the ocean near the pier. I also gave him a complete description of the enchanting Priory School and the kind monks there.

No wonder why the movie stars all love California, like Lucille Ball and Katharine Hepburn and Henry Fonda.

"I didn't see any movie stars, but I loved watching the sun set over the Pacific. We did that a few times. And I put my toe in the ocean as you said."

When do you move west?

"We're not," I said with a smile.

That so? Why? Sounds too good to pass up.

"It's too far. And probably too expensive for us. My grand-mother remains sick and my sister is small. It just didn't feel right for us. I've taken the local job, where I did my practice teaching."

It would have been a great adventure for you, but you are still young, and I will continue to enjoy your visits. Especially if you are teaching history just down the road. You can come back and see us.

He extended his hand as he always did to say goodbye. This time I grasped his hand wearing a wedding ring and as a college graduate. I had grown up. In my maturity, I decided to stay close to my family and the Saint Anselm community rather than wander too far from home.

In July he found one final thing to say about the wedding, which he did by email. As usual, Father Michael offered an accurate observation:

> *July 11, 2002*
> *Dear Jeff:*
> *It is not everyone who has the President of the College and the Dean of the College plus five other priests at their wedding. I had never seen that before. And it had to be a small college to have the President and Dean at a social function.*
> *Father Michael*

II

Adventures

"Let all guests who arrive be received like Christ."

Rule for Monks, Chapter 53

Missing Home

F ather Michael always seemed eager to tell me about his own adventures as well as hear about mine. He especially loved to talk about his visits to Squam Lake in New Hampshire, calling it "the Golden Pond," the place where Henry and Jane Fonda filmed their 1981 movie, *On Golden Pond*. For someone who often reminded me he never traveled far, I frequently found him on the move.

September 12, 2002

Dear Jeff:

On Sunday morning, Father Jude took me and Brother Thomas—who is here in the nursing home with me—and drove us to Squam Lake to see our new boat. It is a pontoon type of boat. The old boat we had was ok, but the older fathers found it difficult to get in and out of the boat. The pontoon type of boat is level with the dock and you just walk into it. It is very large and seats nine passengers. It is not for speed, but for cruising around the lake and watch the speed boats go by. Since the pontoon boat rides on the surface of the water, the speed boats cast waves that rock the pontoon boat up and down. Most of us enjoy it, but any one with motion sickness would not find that very comfortable.

We drove around the lake for about an hour and passed by Church Island. We did not visit this Island, but I had visited it before. The Church is a wide stretch of open land with benches along this area. The reading stand is very nice with the people facing a beautiful stretch of lake. There are many places along the side of Church Island for tying up your boat. Evidently, many attend the Sunday services. Perhaps many attend these services for the thrill of going to church in a boat.

There were many sail boats on the lake and one with a red sail, which reminds me of the song "Red Sails in the Sunset." These pontoon boats are becoming quite popular, four of them passed our cottage while we ate lunch on the porch. There are passenger boats that take tourists for a cruise up the Golden Pond, too. We saw only three, since it was after the season.

Father Michael

He moved calmly and slowly in his nineties and conveyed this feeling along to many through his letters, like this. The words he wrote from the relative solitude of his desk at the Peterson Residence made clear that Father Michael surely missed campus life. In addition to his travelogues, he also sent letters like this one that reminded both his readers, and perhaps himself, of the College happenings:

March 17, 2003

Dear Jeff:

We have 2,000 applicants for this coming September, and we can take in only 500; 1500 students will have to be turned away. We have tried to solve some of this problem by placing three girls in a room. With all the equipment the students bring with them, this is rather difficult today.

How different from the Second World War, when we had only twelve students living on campus. We had no income from the College. We had a community meeting [of monks] and it was the saddest gathering I ever attended. We had no money coming in and we wondered if we could have breakfast because we had not money to buy a loaf of bread. But the following morning when we awoke, we learned that Mr. Daley had died, left us his farm and twenty-five thousand dollars. In 1940, you could buy many loaves of bread with that money. I say a prayer for Mr. Daley every day.

But what saved St. Anselm College in those days was the pilot training program. I taught math to the pilots. I remember teaching them how to find an airplane carrier in the Pacific. This vessel is very large, but in the Pacific Ocean, it amounts to a grain of sand. And if the wind changed, the pilot had to do some very fast mathematics. The calculator in those days was a circular slide rule. I wonder how many of them used the training I gave them.

Many of the pilots came back in later years with their families to show the children "the college that Daddy went to." As that was the only college he attended, it was his.

We have grown a great deal since those days, and think nothing of spending a million dollars to build a new dorm, and recently spending seven million to build an ice hockey rink. And if you have any time off at all, you should come to the college to see the new hockey rink.

Father Michael

I found a second page stuck to the first. When I separated the two, I found them identical—except for the salutation. The second page began with: *Dear Louis and Regina.* I smile every time I see those, and I have retained both pages (with apologies to Louis and Regina for keeping their copy).

* * *

Father Michael loved the College and Abbey he called home for seventy years. While some monks spent years teaching in California or studying in Rome, he only traveled the relatively-short distance to Washington, D.C. and Latrobe, Pennsylvania for further studies. Some might think he saw the world narrowly given his limited travels, but I disagree. The vow of stability he promised at Saint Anselm became a great gift to the College and Abbey and, on the occasions I have returned to the College, I think of Father Michael's own love for the school much like the College Anthem proclaims: *As days go by, and years are lost, our fondness shall not die! For that fair place which stands on the hill so high!*

Another September

Whether as a student or teacher, I have returned to school every September for thirty-five years. I mark time less by the calendar months and more by the academic cycle. I imagine Father Michael similarly thought about time because, in rereading his letters, I discovered he wrote to me early in the semester during the same week for three consecutive years: Monday, September 10, 2001; Thursday, September 12, 2002; and on Saturday, September 13, 2003. During his last years at the Peterson Residence, Father Michael still "went back to school," even if only in spirit.

> *September 13, 2003*
>
> *Dear Jeff:*
>
> *The new college year is well along the way, and the new interest is in the skating arena. After a hockey game, while the ice is still on the floor, there will be ice skating to music. I remember the old roller skating rinks, when we skated to The Skaters' Waltz, etc. How fascinating that was. How different it will be in a large skating arena.*
>
> *You know, there were cows at St. Anselm when I came in the thirties. My job as a chemist was to test the milk of the cows. If a cow had a calf, whether that calf lived*

or ended in the soup in the dining room depended on the butter fat in the mother's milk. If the mother's butter fat was high, that calf would also have high butter fat and the calf would live. That little calf always watched me, knowing that if I made a mistake, she was done.

As you can see from this letter, things have changed at Saint Anselm. There were no girls on campus in those days. Between classes the students went down to the barn to see the cows, and if a student had been to the barn, and he sat beside you in class, you knew he had been to the cow barn. But that was a healthy odor.

I know that story stinks but there was nothing else to write about.

Father Michael

In time, our afternoon conversations turned from my student life to my life as a teacher. He often asked me how I found the profession (I liked it) and whether or not I found the students of good caliber (generally, yes). I always knew Father Michael as a great cheerleader, and he encouraged me to thoroughly prepare for class and to listen to students' needs. Two of his lessons have stayed with me.

First—and I'm unsure what prompted him to make this comment—he told me: *You must never wake a sleeping student. Teachers often think of it as rude, but we can never assume to know what happened to the student the night before.* I've often thought about this comment, and he knew well the teacher's dilemma: the teacher must demonstrate concern for each student without fostering a lax teaching environment. I still strive to achieve this balance, although I'm unsure of my success, and I'm uncertain I show the same amount of compassion for others as did Father

Michael.

His second lesson sounded similar to his first. *You must never rush a student. The student must have every opportunity to succeed, no matter how inconvenient to you.* Again, in remembering his admonition, he kept the well-being of the student in the foreground. While I think most teachers retain a similar belief, bell schedules, interruptions, and fire drills often get in the way of creating the ideal learning environment. Still, if I brought any lessons from my visits with Father Michael into my classroom, I tried hard to place the student at the center of learning and the daily reminder to meet each student with patience and respect. These two simple lessons were given by a master teacher to a novice, and I still cherish them almost twenty years later.

* * *

As with the abundance of Christmas cards Father Michael sent every year, he also kept both current and former students close to his heart at Easter.

April 20, 2004

Dear Jeff:

On Holy Thursday, Brother Thomas and I went up to the monastery for the services in which the Abbot washes the feet of twelve students. These students give up their Easter vacation to spend the Holy Week in the monastery. We were back there again for the Easter Vespers and a wonderful dinner.

Here at the nursing home, they had an Easter egg hunt—surprisingly because everyone here is over eighty. Perhaps we were celebrating a second childhood.

So I pause now, to wish you God's loving blessing in this lovely season of Easter.
Father Michael

I welcomed his Easter blessing then, and I would again today, because it reminded me that no matter how big I found the world, Father Michael remained with me and prayed for me as I grew. I found that Easter particularly meaningful because my grandmother had passed away the previous summer—without having had the chance to receive the St. Maurus Blessing. Nonetheless I rejoiced in her steadfast belief in the resurrection, which Father Michael never let me forget.

A Captive Audience

"He's across the street at Mount Carmel Nursing Home," the smiling receptionist told me. "He said to meet him there. You won't miss him in the lobby."

I laughed as I thanked her, turned, and walked back outside across the street. The thick clouds made the late afternoon even darker and grayer than typical. I thought of how cold Father Michael must have been while crossing the street.

I had never visited Mount Carmel before, and it looked like a small hospital—far less quaint than the home of the Peterson Residence. I didn't have to ask his whereabouts at the desk because, as I stepped into the lobby, I saw an assembly of wheelchairs and heard what I can only describe using Father Michael's own words as "Honky Tonky" music. Some residents clapped while others nodded their head as they listened. I witnessed a gentle scene, with an aged monk—himself a resident of a rest home—still ministering to those younger than himself.

"I'm here for the concert," I told the receptionist, this one less friendly than the previous.

"He told me to watch for you," she said. "The residents get a kick out of him. Feel free to sit with them."

"How often does he do this? I know he plays some songs at the Peterson after dinner, but this is a larger audience."

"This is only the second time. He had the first about a month ago. I'm sure it won't be the last."

I smirked and nodded before walking to the rear of the lobby. The old upright piano needed tuning, and the slightly-chaotic sound reminded me of an old western saloon. He stopped abruptly—with no apparent ending to his song—and stood (albeit less abruptly). I struggled to hear his faint voice across the large room, but I shared in his own joy even at that distance. He told the residents a story, at times making himself chuckle and, in turn, making the audience laugh. Within ten minutes, the assembled offered their applause and, as he reached for his walker beside the piano, I approached him.

I'm glad you made it to my concert, Jeff.

"I am, too. How did you know I would be coming?"

You do come on most Fridays. Today is Friday. Now, the staff will serve root beer floats, would you care for one?

"Yes, that sounds nice. Thank you."

We sat on a sofa and not long after a staff member brought us two plastic cups filled with an old fashioned float.

It's the Honky Tonky music they like. Just as we had in the old days and I played in my family band.

"They enjoyed it," I said. "Very much."

They're a captive audience.

"I agree. I could tell all the way from the back of the room that they liked the music."

Captive because they can't walk out with their wheelchairs.

Although I never enjoyed another of his concerts, I knew they became his last ministry. He often wrote about them in his letters and they clearly gave him great purpose in the twilight of his life of service.

Teacher: First, Last, Always

One Friday afternoon in early spring, I encountered Father Michael sitting on a bench outside warming himself in the sun. I guessed he had appointed himself porter of the Residence—a throwback to his bellhop days on Cape Cod or his later years greeting prospective students in the College's Admissions Office.

It's a small street, but so many cars pass by.

"It looks quiet to me."

Sit here for a while and you'll see what I mean, he pushed. *Once I saw them move a whole house down this street with a big truck and flatbed trailer. That was an amazing sight. You don't see things like that unless you look, though. In the laboratory, you must teach the student to observe or else he doesn't know what to look for.*

"Do you find the days long?" I asked with genuine curiosity.

No. I cannot believe how fast they pass. You'd think time would move slowly here, but as soon as I eat breakfast I feel like it's already time for bed. The older I get, the faster it goes.

"That's because you keep busy," I encouraged him. "With your concerts."

On Fridays, as you know. The Honky Tonky music they like.

"I know the concerts are very popular," I said.

Come inside; the sun is down and it is colder.

I stood up and pulled his walker closer to him, which he took without problem. I held the door open and we walked inside, passing the kind receptionist with whom I spoke at every visit. She smiled at us.

"It's such a nice spring afternoon to sit outside, Father Michael," she said loudly.

Yes, but it is cold now, so I will tell Jeff a story before he goes.

"Very good. Would you like something to drink?"

Ginger ale for us both, please.

I nodded at her and mouthed the words "thank you" as we turned to the right and continued slowly down the hallway and settled into our usual seats in his room.

Father Michael liked to tell me about his life during our visits. That spring, he sent his devoted readers a brief autobiography with the details of his life he considered most important. I'm particularly fond of this letter because he unknowingly wrote it on my birthday.

May 21, 2004

Autobiography

I was born in 1910 and grew up in Lowell, Massachusetts. My young life was uneventful, I worked in small grocery stores but I did play trumpet in the high school band. In 1929, I entered Lowell Textile Institute to study chemistry. During this time, I held a job as a bellhop in the Mayflower Hotel on Cape Cod in Mahomet, just nine miles below Plymouth.

We had a musical family. My mother started us all off on the piano and then switched us to different instruments—myself to the trumpet, another brother to the sax, and the third brother to drums. My sister played piano but we just could not use her as she had no rhythm. We had a chance to play at a hotel on Martha's Vineyard, but we would have to go for the whole summer and my brothers did not want to do that, leaving their girlfriends for such a long time. I would have loved to go as I liked Cape Cod.

While on the Cape, my mother wrote to me that my young brother was to enter the seminary to study for the priesthood. I thought that was very nice as we had no priest in our family. But the more I was thinking of it, I was talking myself into it. I wrote to my mother that I would like to go with him. I had finished three years at Lowell Textile Institute at the time.

My brother and I both entered St. Anselm College to prepare for the seminary. We liked it there and decided to join the monastic community. My brother and I both went to St. Vincent Abbey in Pennsylvania for the novitiate.

I taught chemistry in the prep school which was at the College at that time. My brother taught math, so we were both active in teaching. My brother stayed for three years, but left because he could see he had no vocation to religious life. I proceeded on, was ordained in 1941, and then went to Catholic University of America in Washington, D.C., to do graduate work in chemistry.

During my graduate work in chemistry, I was called back to the College to teach math to fighter pilots who were training at St. Anselm. I taught the pilots for three years, and then returned to the University to complete my work in chemistry. I returned to the College to teach chemistry for forty years, during which time I also taught in the Nursing Department for six years, and then again in the Chemistry Department.

41

During my years teaching chemistry, I went out week-ends to help out in the parishes where I worked for thirty-six years. I preached with stories and was asked by the monastic community to write-up my stories, which I hesitated to do because of the time it would take. But someone said, "do not take those stories to the grave with you," and I went to the computer and typed them up, which I am proud of.

In 1986, I was retired from teaching and, in June of 2001, I was sent here to the Residence because of poor health. I have been here for three years. I type quite a few letters, especially to former students and to keep my fingers trim, and I bang out chords on the piano. The nurses here thought my music was good, and I developed it into a concert, which I give over in Mount Carmel Nursing Home once a month. I also tell them stories and sing to them. They cannot walk out because they are all in wheelchairs.

Father Michael

His points of emphasis remained the same and illustrated what he considered the bright spots of his life: musical summers on the Cape, teaching chemistry at the College, his stories, and his concerts. One phrase particularly stands out to me: "In 1986, I was retired from teaching and, in June of 2001, I was sent here to the Residence because of poor health." In both instances he made clear that he chose neither retirement nor life at the Peterson, and yet he made the most of his situation. Life didn't stop for Father Michael when he "was retired" or "was sent" to a nursing home, and he accepted each transition as the start of another adventure—a lesson I've tried to grasp during the more difficult times of my life.

Chocolate Ice Cream & Whipped Cream

I n addition to teaching, I took on a curious side job as caretaker for an historic mansion. We lived in what were once the staff quarters, conducted weekend tours for the public, and I cut the grass in the summer. Our life appeared atypical for a young couple, but it also gave us a bit of extra cash as we joined the workforce. Father Michael loved every bit of this adventure, and I agreed to drive the hour to Manchester to collect him, bring him back to New Ipswich to see the property, and return him to the Peterson before dinner time.

My little red Ford struggled that summer and needed some engine work. After we set the date for our adventure, however, I dared not reschedule. As I drove to Manchester, the temperature gauge steadily climbed and I feared the engine might overheat. I nursed it as I drove, especially when Father Michael rode shotgun. Thankfully, we traveled without issue, and I did not have to realize the nightmare of breaking down on a country road with Father Michael without a cellphone. Nor did I have to make a phone call to Father William, the abbot's deputy, explaining the situation (although Father William would have found it quite amusing provided everyone returned safely).

While the Barrett House is a full three-stories tall with a ballroom on the top floor, I knew Father Michael and his walker could only see the ground floor. Still, the eighteenth-century parlors, kitchen, and dining room were all laden with period artifacts. The early twentieth-century bathroom added to the rear of the house ended the tour with a surprise.

They were a good looking family, he said as we looked at the Barrett portraits above the mantle and in the hallway. *My father would have appreciated a clock like that*, he continued. *I wouldn't have wanted to cook in a kitchen like this*, he said while inspecting the brick hearth.

The real moment of terror—now humorous on reflection—came in the grand dining room, decorated with its Zuber landscape wallpaper and table set for a banquet. With my back turned to him, I opened the window shades to let in sunlight, Father Michael decided to take a seat on an original Chippendale chair. As he sat, I watched the chair wobble but hold together. I figured the antique would have broken if it was too fragile. Father Michael proceeded to pick up, read aloud, and then move the little sign that read "Please do not touch furnishings" before he admired the porcelain and silverware. I waited for him to pull an eye loupe from his pocket and imagined the moment might end with him on the floor along with a pulled tablecloth and pile of priceless dishware. Thankfully, nothing happened and I offer my apologies to Historic New England for the infraction.

When he described the outing in a letter to his friends (July 29, 2004), he wrote: *The dining room table has the porcelain dishware which comes from China, and a sign asking you not to touch the dishes. There is a fireplace in every room, and those in the front rooms are highly decorated. There are two grandfather clocks in the house.*

After our rest at table, we continued on to the Art Deco bathroom that a later Barrett added to the back of the house. Much as he did in the dining room, he turned to me and said: *Now, if you will excuse me, I have some business to attend to,* as he reached for the toilet tank chain overhead.

The toilet lacked plumbing and I knew this would end in disaster if I didn't intervene. I put myself between his walker and the commode and pointed towards the door.

"The visitor's bathroom is just down the hall and much more comfortable," I reassured him.

Fine, fine, he said, setting off not unlike Mr. Magoo and having avoided another mishap.

* * *

I would like to visit Barrett's grave, if it is convenient, he told me when we rendezvoused.

Fortunately the grave is a short distance from the house and he described the side-trip as such: *Charles Barrett's grave is in the town cemetery with a modest grave stone. We stopped to say a prayer at his grave. New Ipswich is a short distance from the Massachusetts border. The cemetery would indicate that the town is very old.*

For all the comedy of the afternoon, his inclination to visit the grave and say a Latin prayer gave the adventure, like our others, a feeling of serenity and calm. The day presented much for me to manage with the drive, the broken car, and maneuvering him and his walker, but the memories of the dining room chair, the porcelain toilet, and his blessing over the grave while we stood under the leafy green leaves of the New England cemetery all give me much joy today.

* * *

My eyes felt heavy as we drove back into Manchester in the late afternoon.

I should like to go to Blake's for ice cream if you don't mind.

Of course I didn't mind, but with another hour of driving ahead, I also wanted to head home. Fortunately, Blake's is near the Residence and I could let him off at the cafe door while I found parking. I joined him at a booth inside when I entered.

The waitress greeted him with "Hello handsome," but he took it as a fact rather than a tease.

I will have a little dish of chocolate ice cream, please. With whipped cream. And whatever the young man will have.

"I'll have the same, please," I said.

With whipped cream, Father Michael reminded her as he handed her ten dollars before she finished taking the order.

"I'll give you extra whipped cream," she said with a wink.

The nursing students always loved me. He said as she left. *The nurses needed to pass my class, and I helped them until they did.*

Father Michael's stream of consciousness amused me.

He continued to marvel at the contents of the Barrett House and the wealth inside that rural manor.

It's a very good situation you have there. Not many people can say they live in a house like that, and it gives you something to do in the slow summer months.

For all the tiny stressors that day, he was correct; the situation was good and I enjoyed sharing it with him.

"Thank you for the ice cream," I said as we gathered our things to leave. "From cows to computers," I reminded him.

Yes. Cows to computers. It was my pleasure.

Like always, I believed him.

Joy in the Ordinary

E ven when he stayed close to home, Father Michael wrote about ordinary things in a special way. Always a monk, he also lived up to his calling as a chemist into his old age and proved a good observer of the world and the people around him.

February 4, 2005

Dear Jeff:

This is what is going on at the Residence.

At present, we have seventeen priests who are here because they are retired, and most of them in poor health. But they treat us very well, and the meals are good. All our meals are brought over from Mount Carmel Nursing Home as our kitchen has been discontinued. As everything is wheeled over from Mount Carmel we can say we have "Meals on Wheels."

But there is some excitement in store, as the Knights of Columbus from St. Patrick Parish in Nashua are putting on a Super Bowl party on Sunday evening, just before the game. This organization has been very kind to us, they also put on a Christmas party for us. Three from this organization visit us every Monday evening and bring little snacks for us.

But we also have some disappointments. We are about to lose two nurses who have been with us for some time. But recently they received their LPN, one step below the RN. There is no place for nurses of that standing here at this nursing home. One could stay if she would work at night, but her husband does not want her to work evenings.

I still put on a piano concert across the street at Mount Carmel Nursing Home once a month, usually the last Friday of the month. I play a few Honky Tonky tunes, which they call ragtime. And I tell them a religious story, a funny story, and I sing to them—some of the old time melodies, which they know so well. At this affair, they usually serve root beer floats, which I also share with them. The floats attract the large number. However, I continue with my concert, competing with the free ice cream sodas.

I suppose Elvis Presley met with the same disappointments, but he had the good looks to go along with his problem. We concert artists share in each other's sufferings.

But all in all, this is a wonderful place. We concelebrate Mass every morning, and we are all well cared for.

Father Michael

I never heard Father Michael complain about life at the Peterson Residence, although he clearly wished to return to the Abbey. Rather than resign himself to disappointment, he found new ways to minister at his new home, primarily through his concerts but also by maintaining his generous correspondence with others. Although we never discussed spirituality in any great detail, I have every confidence Father Michael often retreated deep into his heart for his own conversations with God in the quiet moments of each day.

In rereading both his letters and his collection of stories, I see Father Michael liked to write about people, both people he observed himself and people he had heard about. This is particularly true about two stories I have included in this book, one about Father Damien—the Pacific priest—and the other about Doctor Smith. Just as Father Michael observed life near him, he also imagined far-off places he never saw. His love of both people and places is something I did not appreciate in my un-traveled youth, but now that I have crossed a bit of the globe, I credit Father Michael with teaching me to both observe and wonder about the world beyond my own yard.

* * *

Father Damien, a Belgian priest, came west by boat across the Atlantic, through the Panama Canal, and into the Pacific Ocean. He was standing at the rail of the ship, looking towards islands, and saw an island of paradise. The captain of the ship came over to stand beside Damien, pointed to Molokai—the Leper Island—and said,

> *"This was an island of paradise until the white men came. They brought with them leprosy, tuberculosis and a venereal disease. It almost wiped out these people off the face of the earth. To save themselves from total extinction, they rounded up all the lepers and took them to Molokai. They dropped them there like sick animals without shelter, clothes, or food."*

When the captain walked away, Damien stayed there looking toward Molokai and thought about how his own people had done such a thing as bring leprosy, tuberculosis, and the other diseases to the island. He decided then and there that he would go to Molokai and work among the lepers.

When Father Damien found that the lepers were, in fact, without shelter, clothes, or food, he went back to the mainland and argued with the officials for lumber, clothes, and rations. Finally, after many arguments, Father Damien was given these things but they were not going to be bothered by that noisy priest again. They passed a law so that anyone who went to Molokai could not return to the mainland again. Damien accepted the sentence and returned to Molokai to live out the rest of his life.

The next man to visit Molokai was Brother Dutton. He was not a brother, but Father Damien always called him as such. Dutton was a military man. He looked stunning in his officer's uniform. He was invited to all the social affairs in Washington; he made a charming figure in his uniform. One day, he went to visit one of his friends in Washington and had to wait in an outer office. He picked up some literature lying there and read about Father Damien at Molokai. He decided to go and work with Father Damien.

Brother Dutton, being a military man, believed in cleanliness on Molokai. He convinced the lepers to paint their houses and grow flowers around their homes. He believed in parades. When one of the lepers died he had a parade to the cemetery. He obtained instruments for those who could play and he made some banners to carry in the procession. He wanted to bring joy into their unfortunate lives.

Brother Dutton heard that the U.S. fleet was crossing the South Pacific and he wired the President to have the fleet come close to Molokai so that the lepers could see the large ships. The President *ordered the fleet to go as close to Molokai as possible. The lepers lined the shore to watch the flotilla of ships go by. The ships fired their big guns as a salute to Brother Dutton. It was a great day on the island. It was not, however, their greatest.*

The greatest day on the island was when their princess came to visit them. She was Princess Regent and would be Queen when her brother died. The princess broke the law that forbade people to return from Molokai. She planned on spending one hour with the lepers, but instead, she spent all day. The lepers showed her their flower gardens. She was quite impressed and said that she would help them. They knew she was sincere. At the end of the day, when she was leaving—as the boat pulled away—the lepers who still had throats sang "Aloha, aloha." The princess was not ashamed to shed tears in front of the crew and those standing near her heard her say: "These are my people, these are my people."

Father Damien died with leprosy. He, the apostle to the lepers, shared their disease. Someday, Father Damien and Brother Dutton may be canonized because they offered their lives to help the poorest of God's poor.

III

Changes

"Before all things and above all things, care must be taken of the sick."

Rule for Monks, Chapter 36

Sad Changes, Happy Changes

On May 20, 2004, my wife delivered a still-born daughter. I remember sitting in the hospital room, holding her tiny body and looking out the window at the cloudless blue sky. My wife and I enjoyed supportive families and employers, good health, and medical insurance to ease the sting of the tragedy. I decided I wanted to grow from the sadness we endured, starting a journey that eventually brought us to Peace Corps service. When I emailed Father Michael to tell him of the sad news, I found his response both brief and kind. He chose not to dwell on the melancholy:

> *June 5, 2004*
>
> *Dear Jeff:*
>
> *I was sorry to hear the sad news of the baby. You have a saint in heaven praying for you. I do hope you accept it as God's will and go on living as you have been the past few years. You are both young and have many years ahead of you. Take good care of that tourist attraction, I would suspect you will meet some lovely visitors this summer. And I hope I will be one.*
>
> *Father Michael*

We shared the joy of graduation and marriage together, now we shared the sorrow of death, too. Perhaps because Father Michael knew his own time drew short, he chose happiness over sadness. I shared in his happiness a year later when he celebrated his platinum jubilee of life in the monastery, which he explained in detail by letter:

August 10, 2005

On July 2nd, I celebrated my seventieth anniversary in the monastery. The abbot wanted to have a big celebration, but I talked him out of it. We had a mass, in which the abbot gave a talk, and a little reception was held out in the cloister.

I have taught chemistry for forty years, and in that time handled potent chemicals and yet lived to be ninety-four—ninety-five in October. Five years away from one hundred and without cancer or heart trouble, I think I will make it. But I get meaner by the year, just think what the nurses will have to put up with at that time.

I was retired from teaching in 1986. I came to this nursing home in 2001, and have been here for four years. They take good care of us, and the meals are good. And if you can put up with the sameness every day, you will enjoy your stay here.

I still give concerts over in Mount Carmel Nursing Home, which consists of piano playing, telling stories, and singing songs. And they cannot walk out on me for they are all in wheelchairs. I cannot tell the success by the number who come as they seem to draw a larger audience when there are free root beer floats.

When the situation here gets dull, I write stories of

events happening that day, like this.

Father Michael

He always mentioned his concerts, which underscores how close they were to his heart. Clearly these moments brought both him and his audiences joy, just as they did to his readers.

I started to change the direction of my life after the loss of our daughter. Having earned a master's degree in history, I decided to move from teaching high school to teaching college. Father Augustine, who served as Dean of the College at that time, generously offered me a part-time teaching position in the College's Humanities program in the year leading up to my Peace Corps service. Indeed, the 2005-2006 school year seemed to be one of the best of my life. Once again, I felt I belonged in the Saint Anselm community. I enjoyed visiting Father Michael more regularly and I certainly enjoyed once again eating in the student cafeteria at Davison Hall. Perhaps Father Michael identified this renewed zeal in his letter at the end of my first semester as a college instructor.

December 28, 2005

Dear Jeff:

How nice to know that you are teaching at St. Anselm College. It must be quite a thrill to teach at a college where you attended as a student. You do not have to introduce yourself to the faculty, they all knew you as a student. And you are going to find it different being on the staff with the other teachers.

I was at a faculty meeting one day when one of the teachers stood up and asked, 'what difference is it to teach in a Benedictine College?' John Julian Ryan, who taught in the English Department, and was quite a character, taught at Harvard, and Notre Dame, stood up and said, 'I have taught in secular colleges and Catholic colleges, but I have never been in a college as here at St. Anselm where the faculty love each other.' I think that was quite a statement.

One Christmas, I attended a party held by the Maintenance Department, and I sensed the same thing there. The workers seem to love each other. And we hold our workers in that department, many of them have worked there for years and years.

I am glad to see that you are taking time to see the world. Do much traveling before you come to a place like this, where you are confined to live indoor. When you are without a car, and have outlived your family, you are very much alone. Many of the patients here are beginning to lose their driver's license, because their eyesight is failing. They are going to miss their cars.

I am interested in your teaching among the poor children in the world. It is a thrill to see those poor children finding a place in the world.

I am down with a nasty head cold and will have to cancel my next concert. This is the first time in two years that I have had to do this.

Fr. Michael, O.S.B.

I traveled far from home when he wrote those words, taking a small vacation in Ireland between semesters. I saw the green hills he mentioned in his wedding advice years earlier. I renewed my zeal for teaching as my new professional adventure began. Father Michael, however, slowed down, as evidenced by his persistent head cold. In our visits and in his letters he began to repeat old stories and wrote more about the past than he did about the present. I found him pensive but never absent minded. Within a month, I received official word we would travel to Morocco to serve in the Peace Corps, and I happily shared the news with Father Michael who always encouraged my adventuring. His writing had become notably brief:

> *February 17, 2006*
> *Dear Jeff:*
> *I envy your trip to Morocco, since I have never been beyond Pinardville. See the world before you come to a place like this. Be sure to take some pictures before returning. Expect some difference from Goffstown.*
> *Fr. Michael*

I did expect some difference from Goffstown. As he suggested years earlier, I had put my toe in the Pacific on that California trip—just under the Golden Gate Bridge while I watched sea lions play in the bay. The moment felt both magical and, at the same time, not for me—at least not then. Ever since, I think of Father Michael when I visit the California coast, either in San Diego or Santa Barbara, Malibu or Monterey. What I could not imagine as a California life in 2002 became a reality in 2020 when I moved to the West Coast. *See the world before you come to a place like this*, Father Michael so often told me. I gladly write that I have.

Whether I headed to California or Morocco, Father Michael encouraged me to go and grow. But Father Michael did not live to read my messages and observations from Morocco, nor did I have the benefit of reading his wisdom when I sweltered under the hot North African sun.

He mentioned coming down with a "nasty head cold" in his December letter and, while he lived on until May, he never recovered to robust health. His cold lingered before turning into pneumonia, but he peacefully passed from this life to the next. *My bags are packed*, he had often told me. While saying goodbye is rarely easy for me, I found no tragedy in his quick death at age ninety-five.

Father Michael was fifty-five years old when Pope John summoned the second Vatican Council while my parents were only six and seven. Mom and Dad hardly recall the old rite but Father Michael worshiped in the Tridentine style for most of his life. Yet, as his writings made clear, he kept up with the times. He embraced computers when they replaced the campus cows. Although he didn't see 100, he saw quite a lot in ninety-five years even if, as he said, he never went "farther than Pinardville."

Father Michael's life spanned seventeen presidential administrations from William H. Taft to George W. Bush as well as nine papacies, starting with Leo XIII and he lived just a few weeks into the papacy of Benedict XVI. He lived through the First World War and took holy orders during the Second; he survived the influenza pandemic of 1919, the Great Depression, the arms and space races, the fight for civil rights, and he comfortably saw the transition from the Twentieth to Twenty-first centuries. Sure, he saw the campus move from cows to computers, but he also watched the College grow from a single building on the hilltop to include numerous dorms—for both men and women—the library, his beloved science and nursing buildings, as well as two gyms, a football stadium, a hockey arena, and most especially, the soaring Abbey Church. His fascination with the physical world included computers and he saw marvelous achievements in physics, medicine, and chemistry. Finally, in his nineties, he returned to his musical roots as he crossed the street to regale the patients at Mount Carmel Nursing Home, those who were more infirmed than he, with his "Honky Tonky" music and his stories. I'm thankful to say he found time to spend with me, too.

Alumni Hall (postcard c. 1910)

I think I last visited Father Michael on a Friday afternoon in March. The kind nurse at the front desk told me he sat in the chapel, a room I surprisingly never visited. I found Father Michael reciting the rosary with the other residents. I quietly took a seat by the door to join them in prayer until they finished. Father Michael sat across the room by a window, warmed by the last rays of afternoon sunshine.

When their devotion finished, the other priests walked out

while I stood to walk towards Father Michael.

"You must be Jeff," said one man in layman's clothes.

I nodded.

"He thought you would come today," the man said. "What gifts you are for each other," and he patted me on the shoulder before walking through the chapel doors.

"Hi, Father Michael," I said softly as I approached.

Jeff. Come sit where it's warm.

That visit was no different from the others. Only in hindsight does it seem special or final. When the sunlight passed behind the neighboring buildings, we walked back to his room, this time more slowly than we had walked that corridor on my wedding day. He put aside his walker—the basket still outfitted with a small flag, bicycle horn, and loaded with assorted papers—and sat in the larger chair near the computer.

My bags are packed, he reminded me.

"You will see one hundred before you know it," I said, trying to reassure him.

Will they teach you to ride a camel in that big desert?

"I hope so, but only God knows."

Only God knows, he repeated with his elvish chuckle.

Moroccans often finish a phrase about the future with the word *"insh'allah,"* meaning "God willing." Never did I have a better example of waiting for Divine will than in Father Michael.

Have I told you the story about Doctor Smith? he asked.

He had. He never repeated his stories, except that he told me of Doctor Smith several times. When I gathered the memories for this project, the story of Doctor Smith was the only one of which I found multiple copies. Clearly, he liked it. Before I could tell him I knew it, he began to tell of the kind doctor with his eyes mostly closed. I cherished his gentle way as I listened one last time.

When he finished, he extended his hand as he always did, saying, *Visit us again sometime, Jeff.*

"I will, Father Michael. I will," I said—but sadly, I never did.

Sausalito, 2021

I'm remembering the moments I've captured in this little book many years later on another trip to San Francisco. This penultimate chapter isn't the end of the story, but I'm pausing here to reflect and to give Father Michael, in turn, the last words of the book.

* * *

"Mike?! MIKE?! I have an iced cappuccino for Mike!" the barista yells out. She means me. I always use the name 'Mike' when ordering at a coffee shop. It's just a thing I do that makes my friends laugh when they hear it. I think I probably do it to keep Father Michael with me day after day, and the barista doesn't know the difference. Using "Mike" is much nicer than those who have the barista yell "Satan" or "Jerk," although some day I'd like to try "Prince Charming."

I take my coffee from the counter and walk across the quiet street to sit on a bench overlooking Sausalito harbor. Across the bay I can see San Francisco shrouded in fog and I find myself near the place where I first put my toe in the Pacific. The weather is a perfectly sunny 70 degrees and the attitude in Sausalito is always, as they say, "chill."

I owe much to Father Michael, although I don't think he'd want any credit for helping me grow. He challenged me to put a toe in the Pacific and although it took me fifteen years to move, I'm now a California resident living far beyond the boundaries of Pinardville. While he didn't travel far over the course of his long life, he's journeyed with me when I rode camels in the Sahara or prayed at Mother Teresa's tomb in Kolkata. I hear his voice remind me about the Pacific whenever I see it and he reminds me that seeing the world and visiting with her people makes us all better souls.

My unlikely friendship with Father Michael also made me a better—a more understanding—teacher. For all his emphasis on studying chemistry, I think I have told quite a few stories in my history classes, which surely stemmed from his influence. I value laughing with my friends, something he and I always did together, and I hope I am a little gentler because of him, too.

At the start of this book, I invited you to think about your own friendships, especially the ones that might not seem typical. Perhaps, like me, you have benefited from a mentor like Father Michael. I hope you cherish these memories, or aim to make more. You may, however, enjoy the opportunity to befriend a young soul as he did for me. I cannot stress the impact such generosity had on me, and certainly will for others, too. I offer no advice here, nor any instructions about these sorts of friendships, but I have written candidly about my camaraderie with Father Michael along with the adventures, joys, and sorrows we shared together in just seven short years. I suppose if you take anything from these pages, foremost I hope you appreciate his wit and character. If you take something else, perhaps take a new or renewed perspective on a friendship dear to your heart.

Father Michael would contentedly sit on this seaside bench with me and marvel at San Francisco and its bridges in the distance. I think he would probably ask why it's called San Francisco and not San Miguel. He would inspect the boats in the harbor and ask if any were headed to Saint Damien's Molokai. The "Honky Tonky" music of the ice cream truck would catch his ear, and he'd chuckle at the child with a chocolate cone walking alongside her impatient grandmother. He would appreciate the gardener sleeping in the shade of a tree and wonder if the passing college students with their phone-sized computers studied chemistry. While the sunshine would make me too hot, he would enjoy the warmth. The splashes of sea lions would stir his imagination as he thought of the fish and great sea creatures below the waves. In all of this and more, Father Michael would see God's gentle hand at work, and he would smile at all he saw.

Parting

I remember hearing the tower bells toll in anticipation of Father Michael's funeral Mass while I proctored my last exam of the 2006 spring semester. I taught two floors above his old office in Gadbois Hall. I had walked in a few of his footsteps that year.

I grew anxious when I read the clock as ten minutes until the hour and a solitary student continued writing her blue book essay. She consistently earned top grades throughout the school year and I expected her to do just as well on this exam. I could hear Father Michael's admonition as I watched the clock tick: *You must never rush a student. The student must have every opportunity to succeed, no matter how inconvenient to you,* he had said. I prayed to St. Michael for patience.

The student finished with three minutes to spare. She apologized as she handed me her blue book, knowing the funeral would start soon.

"You're the priority," I said. "Father Michael would agree."

She smiled, thanked me, and turned right out of the classroom door while I bolted to the left.

The funeral had all the splendor of any liturgy in the Abbey Church, with Abbot Matthew as the homilist and Bishop Joseph Gerry, the past abbot, presiding. The moment both marked the sadness of death and celebrated Father Michael's hope of resurrection.

At the vigil the prior evening, Father Michael laid in repose in the church choir, a space we sometimes shared at daily Mass or evening Vespers, as well as at my wedding. His monastic cowl, which he wore for seventy years, was pulled over his bald head while his stole hung from his shoulders, signifying the burden of Christ's priesthood he carried for sixty-four years.

"See you soon, old friend," I whispered as I knelt by his side and held the rosary beads he gave me on that snowy day. "May the angels and archangels lead you into Paradise."

Asleep in the coffin, he looked as peaceful as at our last meeting when, also with closed eyes, he recited the story of Doctor Smith.

* * *

When Doctor Smith finished medical school, he graduated with great honors. He set up his office in the center of the town. It was the most magnificent office there. The wealthy people flocked to see their promising young doctor. The poor people did not come—not because they could not pay the fee, but because they felt they were not wanted in that magnificent office. Financially, Dr. Smith was doing very well, but spiritually he felt that he was not getting anywhere. He tried to invite the poor people to his office, but they were afraid to come. So, Dr. Smith went in search of the poor. When he heard that some poor person was sick in the town, he went to their home and took care of them. Soon, the poor began to trust him and to love him. They began to come to his office in great numbers. The more the poor people came, the more the wealthy people stayed away. Soon, Dr. Smith was unable to pay his rent and was asked to vacate his lovely office.

What could he do? He had no money. He decided to look for a place in the poor section of the city. He found a room above a barbershop. There was no elevator, but an outside stairway. Dr. Smith put up a shingle that read: "Doctor Smith, Office Upstairs." The poor people found it difficult to climb those stairs, but they came down with a lighter heart. You see, Dr. Smith always had a kind word to say to each of them. He took one day at a time, and worked close to God and close to God's poor.

One morning, the headlines of the local newspaper read of Dr. Smith's death. He was a great loss to the poor people of the city. They all went to the cemetery for his funeral. The poor wanted to put a tombstone on his grave, but they did not have the money to buy one. A man solved the problem: he went to Dr. Smith's office and got that old shingle. He nailed it to a pole and stuck it into the ground, where it read: "Doctor Smith, Office Upstairs." They really believed he was up there with God, for he who had shown so much mercy to God's poor was certain to be given much mercy by the Lord.

www.ingramcontent.com/pod-product-compliance
Lightning Source LLC
Chambersburg PA
CBHW051038030426
42336CB00015B/2929